W9-DDR-539

Saint Francis of Assisi

Saint Francis of Assisi

Gentle Revolutionary

Written by
Mary Emmanuel Alves, FSP

Illustrated by
Patrick Kelley

BOOKS & MEDIA

Boston

Library of Congress Cataloging-in-Publication Data

Alves, Mary Emmanuel, 1945–
    Saint Francis of Assisi : gentle revolutionary / written by Mary
Emmanuel Alves ; illustrated by Patrick Kelley.
        p. cm. — (Encounter the saints series ; 4)
Summary: A biography of Francis of Assisi, focusing on his unique
conversion experience and desire to imitate Jesus as closely as possible.
    ISBN 0-8198-7030-7 (pbk.)
    1. Francis of Assisi, Saint, 1182–1226 Juvenile literature. 2. Chris-
tian saints—Italy—Biography Juvenile literature. [1. Francis of
Assisi, Saint, 1182—1226 2. Saints.] I. Kelley, Patrick, 1963–
ill. II. Title. III. Series.
    BX4700.F69A47   1999
    271'.302—dc21
    [B]   99-24380
                                                    CIP

"P" and Pauline are registered trademarks of the Daughters of St.
Paul.

Copyright © 1999, Daughters of St. Paul

Published by Pauline Books & Media, 50 Saint Pauls Avenue, Boston, MA 02130-3491. www.pauline.org.

Printed in the U.S.A.

Pauline Books & Media is the publishing house of the Daughters of
St. Paul, an international congregation of women religious serving
the Church with the communications media.

4 5 6 7 8   13 12 11 10 09 08

Encounter the Saints Series

Blesseds Jacinta and Francisco Marto
Shepherds of Fatima

Blessed Pier Giorgio Frassati
Journey to the Summit

Blessed Teresa of Calcutta
Missionary of Charity

Journeys with Mary
Apparitions of Our Lady

Saint Anthony of Padua
Fire and Light

Saint Bakhita of Sudan
Forever Free

Saint Bernadette Soubirous
And Our Lady of Lourdes

Saint Edith Stein
Blessed by the Cross

Saint Elizabeth Ann Seton
Daughter of America

Saint Faustina Kowalska
Messenger of Mercy

Saint Frances Xavier Cabrini
Cecchina's Dream

Saint Francis of Assisi
Gentle Revolutionary

Saint Ignatius of Loyola
For the Greater Glory of God

Saint Isaac Jogues
With Burning Heart

Saint Joan of Arc
God's Soldier

Saint Juan Diego
And Our Lady of Guadalupe

Saint Katharine Drexel
The Total Gift

Saint Martin de Porres
Humble Healer

Saint Maximilian Kolbe
Mary's Knight

Saint Paul
The Thirteenth Apostle

Saint Pio of Pietrelcina
Rich in Love

Saint Thérèse of Lisieux
The Way of Love

For other children's titles on the Saints,
visit our Web site: www.pauline.org

Contents

1

Nothing but the Best

Heavy footsteps split the air, shattering the midnight silence. Just as suddenly they came to a halt. The hollow sound of knocking echoed in the street. *Who could it be at this time of night?* the gray-haired maid wondered as she slid back the bolt. The heavy door squealed open, light from within casting eerie shadows around the gaunt stranger who stood in its frame. Before the frightened maid could ask what he wanted, the man delivered his prophetic message.

"Tell Lady Pica," spoke the deep, steady voice, "that unless she leaves the house and goes to the stable, the child cannot be born." He turned abruptly and disappeared into the night. The startled maid closed the door. *Strange, wasn't it,* she thought as she hurried to relay the message. *Maybe he was sent by God!*

"Please, my Lady, do as the stranger said," begged a young servant girl watching by Lady Pica's bedside. "You have suffered much already."

"Yes," Pica whispered in a weak voice. "I will obey the visitor. Call the attendants to help me...to the stable."

No time was lost in carrying the noblewoman from her plush room to the damp stable. Servants made her as comfortable as possible amid blankets and straw. Even more unusual, Lady Pica seemed quite contented to be there.

The rays of a lone candle danced on the stable walls. There was an expectant hush and then...the cries of a healthy, new baby broke the tension.

"It's a boy! A boy is born for Bernardone!" a maid shouted through the mansion halls. "Come and see my Lady's baby!"

The entire household, servants and maids clustered around the mother and child in the stable. "It reminds you of Bethlehem and the Christ Child," spoke an old gentleman, removing his woolen cap.

Everyone wondered about the "why" of it all. But another thought preoccupied all present that night. The baby's father was soon due home from his trip. What would he say? "Oh," one of the servants groaned, "he won't be happy about the stable part. I don't think the man's got an ounce of common blood in him."

Pietro Bernardone scooped his child into his arms. "My son...in a stable? *Never!*" He whirled around. "My son will be a fine merchant! The finest in Assisi!" he bellowed. "Never mention the stable again, do you understand?" The servants bowed and nodded.

"Yes, Sir."

"Of course."

"Never again, Sir."

But what if God had different plans? No one dared to ask.

Signor Bernadone turned back to his wife. "John! You had him baptized John, like John the Baptist in camel skins? Absolutely not! I'm his father and I say he will be called 'Francis,' after the refined and cultured French. I want him to have the best the world can offer; I want him to *be* the best."

"That he will be," whispered the elderly maid. "That he will be—the best in the eyes of the Lord."

2

A Neglected King

Assisi is a small town in North Umbria, Italy. White alabaster houses with their orange tiled roofs glow in the bright sunlight. Steps wind their way around homes and shops in the narrow streets. The majestic Apennines pretend to touch the sky. Summers bring colorful flowers, and winters are a wonderland of ice and snow. Beautiful Assisi is a place where all nature seems to sing the praises of God.

An old washerwoman leaned out her window surveying the town. "Here he comes again," she chuckled, as she saw a smiling teenager heading her way.

Francis looked up. "Hello, Signora!" he waved.

"A song, Francis! Sing a song just for me!" she called out.

"Ah! Signora! Only the best song for you! And in French, of course." Francis tipped his bright red hat and swooped a gracious bow as though the toothless washerwoman were a queen.

"And where are you off to this time?" the woman cackled.

"Nowhere special, just out to have some fun," Francis replied shrugging his shoulders. "And now for your song!"

Walking backwards down the street, Francis began to sing in French at the top of his lungs. (Italian was the language spoken in Assisi, but whenever Francis was especially happy—which was almost always—he sang in French.) The old woman's face broke into a thousand smiling wrinkles. "You clown!" she called after him. "Come by and see me again!"

Francis came to a stop before a run-down church. With another tip of his hat, he whispered politely, "Good morning, my Lord." Staring at the dusty stone steps, he couldn't help thinking of Jesus all alone inside. He put his hands in his pockets and slowly walked away. The Apennines now appeared in full view, looming over the little town. *How beautiful those mountains are!* he thought to himself. *God has made everything so beautiful—just for us. But what have we done for him?* Francis paused again. He turned and looked back at the shabby old church. "Jesus, the King of kings is living there, present in the Holy Eucharist. And look at the condition of the place!" he thought out loud. "Things would be so different if we *really* lived what we believe...if *I* really lived what *I* believe...."

Just then a mischievous little field mouse scurried by. In a minute, Francis was trying to catch him. All his deep thoughts were gone.

The times, unfortunately, were not even half as beautiful as the town of Assisi. It was the late twelfth century, a time of daring knights and chivalry, a time of parties and pleasure. Following the crowd was the thing to do. But the crowd wasn't always going in the right direction. The Ten Commandments, God's laws, were considered ten big obstacles that got in the way of having fun. Life's real purpose of knowing, loving, and serving God was often forgotten in all the noise. Francis forgot it too.

3

DIAMOND-SHAPED PATCHES

Money meant nothing to Francis. That's probably why he spent it so fast. The bolts of material in his father's shop were mysteriously disappearing too. Francis was giving them away. The son of Pietro Bernardone was the most popular—and generous—young man in town.

"Hey! Francis!" a group of his friends tapped on the window of the Bernardone shop. "See you tonight!"

"At nine o'clock," Francis laughed back.

At nine o'clock sharp, he appeared on the doorstep. And what an appearance it was! The tips of his smile almost touched his ears. His dark eyes were talking fun. Tonight, however, he had added something special. Diamond-shaped patches of bright red, orange, purple, green and yellow covered his jester's suit. Francis was king among his friends. And he knew it!

"Look at that outfit!" roared one of his gang.

"I'll bet his tailor stayed up nights with it!" another boy laughed.

The neighbors often lost sleep as Francis and company roamed the streets at midnight, singing and shouting as they went.

"Your Francis is hopeless," they complained to Lady Pica. "You'd think he was the son of a millionaire, the way he acts."

Lady Pica would lower her eyes and answer, "Now he is a merchant's son, but I pray that some day he will be God's son too."

One day a beggar approached Francis when he was very busy in the fabric shop.

"For the love of God, please give me something," the man pleaded.

"Can't you see I'm busy?" Francis snapped impatiently. "Go away!"

The old man quietly left.

Francis suddenly felt ashamed of himself. *Look what I did!* he thought. *If a friend of mine or a rich man had come in, I would have stopped everything and given him what he needed. This poor man came and asked for my help, "for the love of God," and I sent him away!*

Almost before he had finished the thought, Francis snatched up a pair of scissors. He unrolled a bolt of cloth on the counter and snipped off a large piece of ma-

*The neighbors often lost sleep as
Francis and company roamed the streets.*

terial. Abandoning his customers, he raced out the door after the beggar. "Wait! Stop!" he cried. "I have something for you!" When he caught up with the old man, Francis thrust the cloth into his arms and then emptied the money from his own pockets into the beggar's wrinkled hands. Francis knew his father wouldn't be pleased. But he felt strangely happy and peaceful as he walked back to the shop.

4

A SHORT CAREER

"I could take up your trade, Father, but it's not for me. I want to become something great…like a knight or a famous soldier!"

"Fine!" Signor Bernardone boomed. "I'll write to the mayor today. Perhaps he can use you."

Francis's chance came soon enough when Assisi went to battle with the neighboring city of Perugia. Francis enthusiastically joined the squabble.

Hardly had a day's battle ended when Assisi's men were taken prisoner. Discouragement gripped the defeated little army. Only Francis was optimistic about the situation. In fact he was so cheerful that he irritated many of his comrades.

"Francis!" a fellow prisoner snarled, "here we are in the hands of our enemies, half-starved and wounded and you're making jokes and singing in French!"

"The fighting probably got to him. You know, affected his mind," another man broke in, pointing to his head.

But Francis didn't care what anyone said. He really was happy. "Oh, well, it could be worse," he would say. His optimism was "catchy" and soon it began to rub off on the other men. Before their release a whole year later, all of them had become good friends.

While his time in prison hadn't shattered Francis's spirit, it had broken his physical strength. A high fever racked his body. The townsfolk whispered nervously, "The doctor thinks he's going to die." Lady Pica never left his bedside. She prayed every waking hour, "Please, God, spare my son!"

About a year later the fever finally broke. Little by little, new strength surged into Francis's body.

One morning his mother came into his room smiling. "I have good news, Francis. The doctor says you can get out of bed today!"

Francis sat up. It had been so long. "It'll be great to see the town again!" he exclaimed. He climbed slowly out of bed, but before he even made it to the window, his knees started shaking. Lady Pica caught him just in time.

"What happened?" he asked as his mother helped him into a chair.

"You're weak, that's all. Don't try to do everything all at once," she cautioned. "Remember, you've been sick a long time."

Soon Francis managed to get around with a cane. The first day that he felt strong enough, he took a short walk through the village. Everyone was happy to see him again.

"Well, if it isn't Francis! Thank God you're back on your feet," the old washerwoman called from her window.

"You look great, Francis! Keep up the good work," the cobbler nodded as the young man passed his shop.

Francis tipped his hat, smiling at each person he met. But on the inside, he didn't feel at all like smiling. In fact, the more he looked at the ugly cane that held him up, the more he wondered if he would ever be completely well again. Gazing at the distant Apennines, his thoughts wandered. *I used to run to the foot of those mountains…now I can hardly walk. I had so many great times with my friends singing through the streets at night …now it takes so much energy just to breathe…. But soon enough I'll be better and I'll go back to having fun.*

All of a sudden, Francis found himself shaking his head. *No!* he answered himself.

I won't go back to my old fun. Something's different now. I'm different.

Deep in his heart Francis knew he had an important choice to make—for God, or for wealth and pleasures.

5

Decision!

The months passed by. Pietro Bernardone watched his once lively, outgoing son become quiet and withdrawn. He grew worried. "Francis, what are you thinking?" he finally asked one day.

"Just…well…you know…" Francis stuttered, "just about what I should do with my life."

"An excellent thought!" Signor Bernardone agreed, slapping his hands on his knees. "Let's start with what you *want* to do." His father grinned broadly as he thought of all the possibilities. "I'll send you to school. You'll get the best education. You can have anything I can afford to buy."

"I do feel stronger now. And I have the time…" Francis mumbled.

"So, what will it be?"

Francis looked up. "A knight."

"Again?" Signor Bernardone choked down a laugh. He didn't want to discourage his son. After all, at least this was a start.

"Then a knight you shall be!" his father exclaimed.

Signor Bernardone got Francis the best armor and horse that money could buy. When the day came for Francis to leave, almost all of Assisi turned out to wish him success in his new military career. The townspeople cheered him on as he rode off. Signor Bernardone was proudest of all. "*First!*" he said loudly as he stroked his short, pointed beard. "My son shall be *first*."

Riding away from the village that day, Francis came upon a knight who had lost everything in the war. The young Bernardone couldn't help feeling sorry for him. He unclasped his expensive embroidered cloak and unsheathed his shiny new sword. "Here," he offered kindly. "I'd like you to have these." The astonished knight didn't know how to thank him.

Francis spent that evening in the town of Spoleto. Exhausted from hours of riding, he had no trouble falling asleep. Almost as soon as he closed his eyes, he began to dream. Someone was speaking to him.

"Francis," called a mysterious voice, "is it better to serve the master or the servant?"

"...The...master," he answered, groping for the words.

"Then why do you make the servant a master?"

All of a sudden Francis saw himself as he really was, so small, so poor by God's standards.

"My Lord," he asked, "what should I do?"

"Return to Assisi, and you will be told."

Francis awoke and sat up with a start. He slipped out of bed and knelt down. He spent the rest of the night praying and thinking, reliving the dream over and over again in his imagination.

"God is the only real Master," he murmured. "He alone deserves my life and my love. He must be my King. I will be his knight. God...only God...God...only God."

When dawn broke Francis was ready to leave. If God wanted him to return to Assisi, then he would do just that, and as fast as he could. On the way home, he stopped and sold his armor.

Pietro Bernardone who had so proudly bragged about his son just a few days before was absolutely humiliated to see Francis home so soon. He flew into a rage when he found out that Francis had also given away and sold all the expensive military equipment he'd bought him. Lady Pica was able to calm him down, but Signor Bernardone's anger still smoldered.

Francis's friends brushed the incident off

as another one of his whims. They were happy to have their "king" back and threw a big party for him. Francis went, or at least, he started to go. He was at the head of the crowd as his friends led the way down the street. A few yards later, he found himself in the middle of the group. Minutes after, he was straggling at the end. The noisy group ahead of him disappeared around a corner. He was alone. Francis began to pray, unaware of time, or place, or people. A few of his friends finally noticed he was missing and returned to find him. He didn't even realize they had come back until one of them poked him in the shoulder.

"Hey, Francis! What's wrong with you?"

"I know," another teased, "he's in love."

"You're right," Francis grinned.

"Hope it works out as well as your military career did," someone laughed.

Francis's face suddenly flushed with anger. He turned and walked away, leaving his friends totally confused. He wasn't angry with them. He was angry with himself.

"I've wasted so much of my life," he sighed. "I have to change now. It's God I want to love and serve. Not money. Not fun." And Francis prayed. He really prayed.

6

My Friend, the Leper

The village Church of San Damiano (Saint Damien) and a dingy cave became second homes to Francis. He spent hours praying there. His generous and joyful heart was now determined to seek only God.

Back at home one day his mother found him preparing everything for an extravagant dinner. "What are all these fine linens, dishes and silverware for? A party with your friends?" Lady Pica asked in surprise.

Francis nodded happily. "I've invited all my *new* friends to a party tonight."

"Your new friends?" his mother asked inquisitively.

"Yes, and they're very good friends, too," Francis added.

That evening, Lady Pica peeked in on the party. Imagine her surprise when she saw all the poor, the beggars and outcasts of Assisi enjoying a fine banquet with her son!

Francis had always loved everyone. Now he wanted to grow in love. He wanted to love persons regardless of whether they were rich or poor, kind or cruel, because he saw Jesus in each of them. God soon gave him the chance to prove his love.

One afternoon Francis went riding beyond the gates of the town. Suddenly his horse reared. Up ahead, by the side of the road, sat a leper. Leprosy is a disease that causes body decay. In those days there was no cure for it, and it meant slow and certain death. Everyone was afraid to go near the lepers because the disease was also very contagious.

Francis pulled a few coins from his pocket. He was ready to toss them to the leper when he had an unexpected thought. *This poor man is loved by God just as much as I am. He really is my brother because we're all God's children.*

Gripping the horn of his saddle, Francis dismounted. Slowly he walked toward the leper. With every step the sickening odor of rotting flesh became stronger. He had to force his legs to keep moving. Francis swallowed hard. His stomach was feeling sick.

I have to keep going. I have to show God that I want to love him without limits. I have to show this man that I love him and care about him. With all his heart Francis took the last step.

The leper crouched in fear. He didn't know what to make of this rich, healthy young man who dared to come near him. His sore, red eyes opened even wider when Francis pressed the coins into the palm of his hand and kissed him, putting his arm around the leper's shoulder as if they were best friends! Not a word passed between the two. But God was speaking in their hearts.

Minutes later the poor leper sat stunned, staring at the coins in his hand. Tears streamed down his cheeks. Francis was already back on his horse, riding down the road with a heart so full of joy that he thought it would burst.

7

THE UNWANTED GIFT

Francis knelt before the dusty crucifix in the Church of San Damiano. "God, please tell me what you want me to do," he begged. A voice seemed to penetrate the silence, echoing deep within his soul. "Francis, Francis...." Young Bernardone remained motionless. Was Jesus speaking to him? His eyes riveted on the crucifix, Francis listened with his heart.

"Francis, go and repair my house," the voice directed.

At last Francis had a specific mission to accomplish! He was ready to throw himself into the work. There would be no half measures in serving his King. The youth scanned the cracked walls of San Damiano's and noticed the gaping holes in the roof. He headed straight for his father's store.

A short time later, Francis was on his way to the market, his horse loaded down with the finest rolls of Oriental fabric which he had whisked away from their shelves. Late that night the young merchant re-

"Francis, go and repair my house."

turned home in triumph, singing in French. Not a single yard of material was left. Neither was his horse. He had sold it, too!

The next day Francis returned to San Damiano's. He found the church's elderly priest sitting by the door. "Father, here it is —everything you need to repair the church!" he exclaimed, waving a bag of money in front of him. The priest raised his eyebrows. "Where did you get it?" he asked in amazement.

"I sold some material."

"You must have sold *quite a lot* of material, and without your father's permission too, because he isn't even home!" The priest shook his head. "I'm sorry, Francis. I can't accept it. I know your father too well. He won't be pleased."

"But I work for him. I'm his son. This is only my share. Take the money, Father," Francis pleaded. "It's for the church." The old priest silently shook his head.

Francis looked up at the dilapidated building and then back down at his unwanted gift. Shrugging his shoulders, he started to walk away. He took a few steps then stopped. "Won't you reconsider, Father?" Again the priest sadly shook his head.

"But it's for the church," Francis muttered to himself, "and it's only *my* share." He bounced the bag up and down in his hands and turned with determined steps toward home. But he just couldn't do it. Why *should* he take the money back? It was meant for God. He ran and dropped the sack onto the priest's windowsill. *Just in case he changes his mind.* He put his hands into his pockets and left. It was time for a song now....a French one, of course.

The first thing Signor Bernardone noticed when he returned home was that some of his shelves were empty. Francis was missing, too. Knowing his son, it didn't take him long to put two and two together. "Where is he?" he roared. "Where *is* he?"

Lady Pica tried to calm him down. "It can't be that bad, Pietro."

"It *is* that bad, and I can just guess *where* he is," he bellowed, slamming the door behind him.

The priest at San Damiano's saw Signor Bernardone coming. He knew he would have to watch his words.

"Hello, Pietro. You're back from your business trip I see," he began with a nervous smile.

"Where is he?" Signor Bernardone demanded.

"Who?" the old priest asked "Do you mean Francis?"

"Who else?" the merchant retorted angrily, "I want my boy, and I want my money—now!"

"Yes, well...the money is all here." The priest's trembling hand reached for a little bag hidden carefully behind the door. He handed it to Signor Bernardone.

"He means well..."

"Keep your excuses to yourself, priest!" Bernardone snapped.

Later in the day, Francis slipped into San Damiano's. The priest told him what had happened. Francis lowered his head. "I'm so sorry, Father. I didn't think it would turn out this way. My father has so much...and gives God so little."

The old priest rested his hand on Francis's shoulder. "When you look for your treasures on this earth, that's where your heart remains," he said kindly. "Heavenly treasures are much harder to understand, but 'when a man finds that single pearl of great price, he sells all that he has to buy it.'"

Francis understood. God was that pearl of great price. He would search for God. He would give up everything he had to follow him without reserve. Yes, *everything*.

8

Bread, Water and Brother Ashes

"Look! A crazy man! A crazy man!" the children taunted, pointing to a slight figure sitting by the side of the road. Townsfolk peered through their shop windows to see what all the commotion was about. To most, the young stranger appeared to be just another beggar. But one elderly townsman who had gotten a closer look wasn't as convinced. He stood there scratching his head, and each stroke of his fingers through his thin, white hair, seemed to bring him closer to a conclusion.

"Looks like the fellow hasn't slept for a week...pale face, black eyes, underweight ...but if that's not Francis Bernardone, this isn't Assisi!"

Francis was back! The news raced through the village, quickly reaching the Bernardone palace. "My Francis, a crazy man?" Signor Bernardone repeated in disbelief. He ran out into the square pushing his way through the crowd of children. "So, it's true!" he shouted, as he came face-to-face with his son. Grabbing Francis by the arm he dragged him home and threw him into the cellar.

"Stay there, stay there!" Signor Bernardone screamed with the little voice he had left, "and bread and water is all you'll get!" He slammed the cellar door and locked it.

"That will break him," the bewildered man said to himself, "all this nonsense about fasting, praying and strengthening his spirit—I can't believe it. Either he's crazy or I am! A little time in the cellar will do him good."

A few days later, Signor Bernardone went off on a business trip. Francis heard the cellar door creak open. He squinted up into the light coming from the doorway. Lady Pica was hurrying toward him with a steaming tray of food.

"It's your favorite dinner, Francis," she said gently.

"Be careful, Mother! What if he sees you?"

"Don't worry. Your father is away for several days," Lady Pica responded with a smile. "This foolishness has gone on long enough," she continued, shaking her head. "And it's all because your father doesn't understand your prayers and penances." She paused. "But maybe you could compromise a little, Francis. Go to a few parties, and get interested in the fabric shop again."

Francis smiled at his mother. Then his face grew serious. "My way now is to follow Jesus. Peace is never found in compromise with the world."

Lady Pica had no answer. She knew her son was right. She gestured toward the tray. "Eat something, Francis, you must be hungry and the food is getting cold."

Francis picked up a slice of bread, dipped it in water and sprinkled it with ashes from the floor. Lady Pica gasped, "What are you doing?"

Francis's pale face flushed red. He had become so used to this penance that he did it now, forgetting the presence of his mother.

"It's just a little sacrifice," he explained. "It helps me to grow in the love of our Lord. 'Brother Ashes' helps keep my mind and body strong and pure."

Lady Pica could see that Francis had changed. Her fun-loving, worldly son was now becoming that "son of God" for whom she had so often prayed. Her throat tightened and her eyes filled with tears. "No one else is home," she whispered, taking Francis's hands in her own. "Leave while you have the chance. Follow the path God has chosen for you, and know that your mother follows you with her heart wherever you go."

Francis said nothing. His eyes thanked her. He kissed his mother gently on the forehead and climbed the stairs to freedom.

9

OUR FATHER

The "cell" was empty when Signor Bernardone returned home. His plan had failed miserably. But Pietro wasn't finished with Francis. If his son wouldn't obey him, then he would disown him. Signor Bernardone turned the matter over to his lawyers, who summoned Francis to civil court. There he would be publicly disinherited from the entire Bernardone estate. Francis didn't obey the summons because he felt that his case had to do with a religious, not civil, matter. Then his father brought the matter directly to the bishop. Soon after, father and son met in the bishop's courtyard. A crowd of priests and onlookers had gathered to see the outcome.

"Your Excellency," Signor Bernardone began, "the shameful conduct of this young man has disgraced our name. From this day on, I no longer consider him my son. I demand that he return anything he has gotten from me!"

The silence was deafening. Francis removed a small bag of coins from his belt. He set it down before his father. A shocked murmur ran through the crowd as Francis next began removing all his clothes, piling them in a heap at his father's feet.

"Here is everything, Father. All that you have given me, I return." Francis looked from face to face as he spoke. "Until today, I have called Pietro Bernardone 'my father,'" he said loudly, "but from now on in all truth I shall say only, 'Our Father, who art in heaven.'"

Many had tears in their eyes. The bishop, too, was moved. But Signor Bernardone was furious. His face was red and his breathing heavy. He could see his son only as a rebel. And, in a way, he was right. Francis was a rebel, but not in the way his father thought. His "rebellion" was against the lifestyle of a world that refused to pay attention to God. His all-powerful weapon in this rebellion would be total, self-sacrificing love and dedication to Jesus and his Church.

Signor Bernardone silently scooped up the clothes and the money and walked away. But his son's prayers would follow him, and someday he would understand. The bishop stepped forward and put his hand on Francis's shoulder, spreading his own cloak around him. The last thread tying the young man to his past life was cut.

Francis was free at last. But the freedom he had won was not something selfish and private. He wanted to give everything he had to God. He wanted to help other people in every way he could. Francis looked at the world around him and saw that many things were not the way they should be. He wanted to build a world of goodness. And he knew God would help him.

Francis walked slowly out of the courtyard. He felt stronger, happy, because this day marked the beginning of a whole new life. He would pray hard to know what God wanted next.

10

HERALD OF THE KING

"Who goes there?" The reeds along the side of the lonely road came alive as a band of robbers jumped out from behind them.

"Halt!" they shouted, pointing swords at Francis. "Who are you?" the leader demanded.

"I am the herald of the King," Francis responded calmly. "I'm on my way to the village of Gubbio. May I be of some service to you?"

The robbers exchanged sly glances and snickered at their odd-looking victim. Francis was dressed in a shabby gardener's cloak. His hair was uncombed and he was barefooted.

"Herald of the King, eh? What kind of king would claim you?" The bandits laughed loudly. At their leader's signal, four of them stepped forward. Grasping Francis's legs and arms they tossed him high into a snowbank. Still laughing, they went off in search of more prosperous clients.

Francis pulled himself out of the snow and briskly rubbed his arms. He continued down the road, singing. Soon enough the monastery of Saint Benedict came into view. The kind monks there offered him hospitality. He remained with them for a few weeks praying and thinking. Leaving Saint Benedict's, he continued on to Gubbio. There a friend gave him a hermit's tunic, leather belt, shoes and a staff. Francis spent every spare moment serving the lepers in the nearby hospital.

Then...it was back to Assisi and the Church of San Damiano.

11

STONES FOR THE LOVE OF GOD

I don't have the money to have a new church built here, Francis thought, *but who says I can't build it myself? The next problem is, where can I get the mortar and stones?* He rubbed his chin. *Well, if God wants a new church, he'll have to provide.*

"Stones! Stones...for the love of God!" Francis called out as he walked up and down the streets of Assisi. "Whoever gives me a stone will have a reward from God. Whoever gives me two stones will have two rewards from God."

There was no doubt that Francis had always possessed a strong pair of lungs, and once again he put them to good use.

He soon became quite an attraction, piling stones and mixing cement with almost as much perspiration as water. Of course he also sang as he worked. Passers-by who stopped to admire the project received a kind invitation to help. Some only laughed, and Francis laughed with them. Others were moved to tears to see the son of a wealthy merchant in such a condition.

"Ask Francis if he'll sell you a dollar's worth of sweat," Francis's brother Angelo joked to another boy.

Overhearing him, Francis answered cheerfully, "I've already sold it—and at a good price—to my King."

As the old pastor watched the stones slowly reconstruct his church, he couldn't do enough to show Francis his gratitude.

"Tell me if there's anything more you need, Francis, anything."

"I appreciate your concern, Father, but the Lord is taking care of everything. This is the least I can do for my King."

Finally the work at San Damiano's was finished. Francis left behind enough oil to keep the sanctuary lamp always burning before the Blessed Sacrament. Then he moved on to begin repairing the Church of San Pietro (Saint Peter), not too far away.

"This is the least I can do for my King."

12

To Be an Apostle

The Chapel of Santa Maria degli Angeli (Saint Mary of the Angels) was Francis's next project. In no time he had it restored to its former beauty.

One morning, on the feast of Saint Matthew, apostle and evangelist, Mass began as usual in the chapel. The Gospel of the day was taken from Saint Matthew. The priest read clearly and slowly: "Jesus sent these men on mission...after giving them the following instructions.... As you go, make this announcement: 'The reign of God is at hand!' Cure the sick, raise the dead, heal the leprous, expel demons. The gift you have received, give as a gift. Provide yourselves with neither gold nor silver nor copper in your belts; no traveling bag, no change of shirt, no sandals, no walking staff. The workman, after all, is worth his keep. Look for a worthy person in every town or village you come to and stay with him until you leave. As you enter his home bless it. If the home is deserving, your blessing will descend on it. If it is not, your blessing will return to you" (Matthew 10:5–13).

That morning the Gospel touched Francis in a special way. He was sure that God had spoken especially to him through the inspired words of Matthew.

As soon as Mass was over, he asked the priest to explain the reading to him word by word.

"There must be no compromises with God," Father said. "His servant must be poor in spirit and possessions. Whoever really wants to follow Jesus must preach the good news of the Gospel to all people and live it well himself."

"This is what I want!" Francis exclaimed excitedly. "This is exactly what I want to do with my life!"

The priest was impressed by his sincerity and gave Francis his blessing.

Francis exchanged his hermit's robe for a gray tunic like those worn by peasants and his leather belt for a rope. He removed his shoes and staff and walked from town to town, preaching about Jesus to anyone who would listen. Francis, God's herald and church builder, was now Francis the apostle.

13

Brothers in Christ

What if this is just another one of Francis's crazy ideas? He's had so many of them. Bernard of Quintavalle sat down to think. He planted his elbows squarely on the table and rubbed his temples with his hands.

Crowds were flocking to hear Francis preach. And many were being drawn closer to God by his good example. Other young men who had watched him change from a happy-go-lucky party-goer to a man of God were now really interested in what he had to say. The truth was, Francis was actually keeping to the strict religious life he had designed for himself. Bernard wondered about it all.

Francis was no great speaker. But something was attracting people to him. There was a mystery about him that some called "madness." While his peaceful expression hid the fire that burned in his soul, his dark eyes penetrated the hearts of all who met him. "The Lord give you peace," was always his greeting. His only desire was to share the grace and peace of Jesus with the whole world. Francis wanted to love Jesus and make him loved.

"Repair my house," Jesus had told him. Francis knew now that Jesus had meant, "Help people to welcome me into their hearts."

Bernard was lost in thought. *Maybe Francis is on the right road. Could it be that God is calling me to the same life?* The young nobleman prayed for guidance. True, Francis's way of life was found in the Gospel, but Bernard had to *really* be sure before he took any decisive step. He just had to be sure. Suddenly an idea crossed his mind. *That's it!* he thought to himself. *I'll find out what he's really like.*

Bernard found Francis at the end of a day of preaching. "Francis, would you honor me by staying at my house this evening?" Bernard asked.

"Of course," Francis accepted with a smile. "It will be wonderful to spend some time with an old friend."

The two men talked until the early hours of the morning. When they finally went to bed, each only pretended to be sleeping. Francis opened one eye, then the other. When it looked as if Bernard were sleeping soundly, Francis quietly slipped out of bed and began to pray. He prayed all night long, climbing back under his blanket just before sunrise. Little did he know that Bernard had not slept either. Through the corner of his eye, he had been watching every move Francis made. Now Bernard was convinced that his friend was sincere. And now he was determined to follow him. Later that morning Bernard asked, "Francis, if a man received many goods from his master, and then decided he didn't want them, what should he do?"

"Give them back, of course!" was Francis's quick reply.

Bernard's smiling face grew serious. "Francis, I want to return to God all the earthly possessions he's given me. What should I do?"

Francis thought for a moment. He laid his hand on his friend's shoulder. "Tomorrow we'll go to church together and pray for the answer to your question."

14

A RULE

Before that tomorrow arrived, a brilliant lawyer, Peter Catanii, joined the two men. The following day all three knelt before the altar at the Church of San Nicola (Saint Nicholas) near the city square. Francis opened the large missal that contained the four Gospels. He read the first passage he found. It was Jesus speaking to the apostles: "If you will be perfect, go sell what you have, and give to the poor and you will have treasure in heaven."

He opened the book a second time, and once again read the first passage his eyes fell upon: "If any man would come after me, let him deny himself, take up his cross, and follow me."

A third time Francis opened the book and read: "And he commanded them that they should take nothing on the way!"

Francis looked up. "Brothers," he said, "this is our rule. We must now go and do what we have heard."

As soon as they left the church, Bernard

and Peter returned home, collected all their possessions and gave them away to the poor. Then they walked to the Chapel of Santa Maria degli Angeli where they joined Francis. Together they built their first home, a clay hut. They called themselves the "Little Brothers." (Another common word for "brother" at that time was "friar.") Father Francis, as the brothers now called him, was their leader and father. It was the beginning of what would come to be known down through the centuries as the Franciscan Order.

15

ONE BY ONE

"I saw it with my own eyes…right there on the church steps! Bernard and Peter gave away all they owned!"

The gossip buzzed loudly over the crackling fire in the square. When Francis had left everything to follow Jesus, he had been the talk of the village for weeks. Now, about two and a half years later, two other prominent citizens had joined him. What was it all about?

"That's nothing," another piped up. "I even heard that they're living in a hut near Santa Maria's."

Heads were shaking back and forth. There was a silent pause. Then an elderly woman spoke up.

"I was there twenty-seven years ago when Francis was born. A stranger came to the door and told Lady Pica to go to the stable or the child would not be born." Some in the crowd were straining to hear what the old woman had to say. "It was like the first Christmas in Bethlehem," she went on. "I knew from that day on that God had special plans for that child. Maybe those men aren't as crazy as you think."

Her audience wasn't easily convinced.

"No house, no food, no money, and you say they aren't crazy?"

The old woman stood her ground.

"They have the courage to give all to God. They have peace and joy and the blessings of the Lord. I say they are wiser and richer than many of us."

In the background, a silent young listener was taking careful note of the whole conversation. The old woman made sense. Francis made sense. After a restless night, this same young man set out for Santa Maria's. As he approached, he saw a familiar, gray-clad figure in the distance.

"Brother Francis!" he called, running to catch up with him. "Brother Francis, wait!" Francis stopped and waved.

"Father Francis," the youth panted as he reached him, "my name is...my name is Giles. With all my heart...I want to serve God. Please...let me be one...of your brothers."

Giles' simplicity and sincerity impressed Francis. "God has been very good to you, my Brother," he said with a smile. "Let's say a prayer of thanks together."

Francis and Giles returned to the hut where Brothers Peter and Bernard were busy with chores.

"Bernard! Peter! I have good news!" Francis stood smiling at the doorway with Giles behind him.

"What, Father Francis?" they questioned curiously.

Stepping aside, Francis pulled Giles to his side.

"God has blessed us with Giles, another brother to share our joy and our labor."

"Welcome, Giles!" Peter enthusiastically cried.

"We're happy you've come!" echoed Bernard.

Giles felt right at home. Many more young men would soon follow him, one by one.

16

Prayer, Penance, Preaching

"We're men from Assisi, who live a life of prayer, joy and penance." This was the answer the brothers gave to anyone who asked about their life. Just as Jesus had sent the apostles, Francis and his followers went out two by two preaching the Gospel in the surrounding towns and villages. Some people received them well, others didn't. But nothing discouraged Francis and his brothers, who had picked up his joyful spirit. All they wanted was to love Jesus and to make him loved.

More men came to join the Little Brothers. Sabbatino, Morico and John were three of them. Before they left on their missionary journeys, Francis would call all the brothers together. He encouraged them by reminding them of things Jesus had said in the Gospels. "Be patient and humble, Brothers. Preach the Good News of Jesus to everyone. Stay where you are sent for a time and accept whatever is given you." At the end of his little talk Francis would happily remind them, "And rejoice, because your names are written in heaven."

The Little Brothers imitated the very first apostles of Jesus. First of all they prayed. From their communication with God they received the grace and help they needed to go out and bring Jesus to others. God sent more men to join them: Brothers Philip, John, Barbarus, Bernard of Vigilanijo and Angelo. Soon they were twelve, just like the original apostles. The hut they called home was now too small. They found a shed at a spot called Rivo Torto (Twisted River) and it became their new "friary." It wasn't much of an improvement, but at least they were all together. "Here is your room, Peter. And yours will be over here, Barbarus." Francis smiled as he marked off each "room" with a simple chalk line drawn on the floor. On the twelve beams supporting the shed, he wrote the names of each of the brothers to designate their quarters.

The Little Brothers could be found wherever help was needed. They worked in hospitals. They cared for lepers. They lived the life of God's poor. They were paid with the bread they ate, but when even bread was scarce, the roots of herbs and grass served just as well. Each night the sound of the brothers chanting their joyful praises to God echoed from the humble shed, reaching the village and touching the hearts of all who heard it.

As more and more men joined, Francis began to realize that a new religious congregation was forming around him. He decided that they shouldn't go one step further without first obtaining the blessing of the Pope. He called the brothers together. "We're going to make a pilgrimage to Rome," he announced. "There we'll pray at the tombs of Peter and Paul, the first apostles, and ask the Holy Father's permission to preach and continue our life of prayer and penance."

With great excitement the brothers left Rivo Torto for Rome. The hours of the long journey passed quickly as they prayed, sang and relaxed together. The year was 1210. Francis was twenty-eight years old.

17

"GOD WILLS IT"

A small band of men, dressed in shabby gray tunics approached the Eternal City. "Who are they?" passersby murmured, as they stopped to stare at the unusual group. The brothers, used to every kind of reaction from people, peacefully went on their way.

After a visit to the tombs of the apostles Saint Peter and Saint Paul, they unexpectedly met Bishop Guido from Assisi, who also happened to be in Rome. The bishop was surprised to see the Little Brothers. Upon learning the reason for their pilgrimage, he arranged for them to meet with Cardinal John of Saint Paul, who could make a visit to the Holy Father possible.

The reaction of the cardinal matched that of the Roman people: he wasn't exactly sure what to make of the barefoot troop. *They really look more like beggars than brothers of the Church*, he thought to himself.

"Come back tomorrow," said the bewildered cardinal. He needed time to learn more about this new community.

It's easy to understand the cardinal's reaction. The times were very troubled. Some people resented authority, even the authority of the Pope. Some of the priests were caught up in worldly affairs, too, and the faith of Christ's people suffered.

Cardinal John drummed his fingers on his desk. "How does the little man from Assisi fit into all this?" he mumbled to himself. "I wonder."

"But Bishop Guido," the cardinal's tone changed from pleading to sarcasm, "absolute poverty and the preaching mission, too? The man is crazy. Monks embrace poverty and priests preach—one man cannot do both! If they are going to preach, they will need financial support and..."

Bishop Guido interrupted, "I assure you, Your Eminence, that Francis's way of life will work. He is sincere and loyal to the Church and to the Holy Father. All he wants is to lead the world to God. Speak to him. See for yourself."

Francis and his brothers were called to return to the office. "Poverty and preaching? It's too idealistic," Cardinal John argued, as he paced back and forth. "How do you plan to keep going?"

"The life we seek is written in the Gospel, Your Eminence," Francis respectfully answered. "If the apostles could live it, I believe God will give us the same grace. He has even sent us brothers."

The cardinal fell silent. *Yes. Yes, it's true,* he thought to himself. *This young man has the courage and devotion to* really *live the Gospel.* He rested his hand on Francis's shoulder. "God bless you, Brother Francis. I will do what I can. I will arrange a meeting with His Holiness."

Francis and his brothers returned to the tombs of the Saints Peter and Paul. They prayed and waited....

The next day, they came to the appointed place. Again they waited. Time had never passed so slowly. Finally, a door swung open.

"His Holiness will see you now," a priest announced.

In through the large door the brothers quickly filed with Francis in the lead. They found themselves in a great hall. When Francis saw the Pope only a short distance ahead, his feet came to a sudden stop. The fact that they were actually there suddenly struck him full force.

"Come," the Holy Father motioned with a smile. "What is it you seek?"

Pope Innocent III listened carefully as Francis explained his way of life. The Pope appeared to be deep in thought and said nothing for a long time. At last he raised his eyes. "My son," he said kindly, "I am afraid that your life is too severe. I am convinced of your good will and strong spirit, but what about those who will follow you later?"

Francis fixed his gaze on the large, wooden crucifix that hung from the wall. "Your Holiness," he responded humbly, "I depend on my Lord Christ. He, the Creator of heaven and earth, will give us what we need. He himself has said, 'Seek first the kingdom of heaven and all else will be given you besides.'"

A fatherly smile lit the Pope's face.

"Yes, and he also said, 'the spirit is eager, but the flesh, weak.' Pray therefore to see how far God wants you to follow in this way."

The meeting was over. Francis and his brothers went away...to pray....

18

A Dream?

The Pope's days were filled to the brim with all the usual affairs of the Church. But at one point his priest aide noticed that the Holy Father didn't look well.

"Your Holiness, may I help you in any way?" the aide asked.

"No, no, Father," the Pope replied with a slight smile. "I'm just tired. I was awake half the night. I kept having the same dream over and over, and each time it woke me from sleep."

The Pope's face became troubled as he relived the dream. "I could see a church shaking. Some bricks even began to fall from it. I saw myself in great sorrow over the problem of heresy and I wept as I looked at the confused faces of many of Christ's people." The Pope stopped and put his head in his hands.

"Then what?" the priest gently prodded.

"Then, just when the whole church was ready to crumble, a small man came up to it. Making the sign of the cross, and putting his shoulder to the front of the building, he kept it from falling."

"The dream had a good ending, Your Holiness," the priest encouraged.

The Pope seemed not to hear him. "That face," he murmured, "the face of the little man. I've seen it before—but where?" He looked up at the clock.

"How many more audiences are scheduled, Father?"

"Just one, Your Holiness, the one with the man from Assisi."

"Who?"

"You remember, Brother Francis and his followers."

"Oh, yes, I vaguely remember. Please show them in."

When Francis and the brothers entered the hall, Pope Innocent stood up in surprise.

"Is something wrong, Your Holiness?" the aide asked.

"It's the little man!"

"Pardon me?" the puzzled priest responded.

"That's the man!" the Pope continued.

"Yes, the one from Assisi, Your Holiness," the confused aide repeated.

"He is the man who kept the church from falling in my dream!"

The Pope didn't wait for the brothers to approach him, but walked briskly across the great hall and met them half way. Not for a minute did he take his eyes off the serene face of the young man who led the group.

"Your Holiness," Francis began humbly, "God has given me these brothers to follow the way of penance and prayer revealed to us in the Gospel. Will God, who has so blessed our community, refuse to give us what we need spiritually and materially?"

The Pope's eyes filled with tears. A thought flashed through his mind. *This man will restore the Church.*

The Holy Father embraced Francis. "Go, my son," he said quietly, "with your good brothers. May God be with you. Preach the Gospel and continue your life of poverty. When God blesses you with more brothers, return, and we will help you continue along the paths the Lord will trace for you. You have our permission, and our blessing!"

19

THE SPIRIT OF JOY

The Little Brothers joyfully returned to Assisi—only to find that they were homeless! A farmer had claimed their shack at Rivo Torto as his own property. Francis, with his usual optimism, turned the problem upside down.

"How kind God is!" he exclaimed to the brothers. "Our house was too small, so he took it away. Now our good Father will give us something even better."

And he was right. The Benedictine monks offered the little group a bigger home near the Chapel of Santa Maria degli Angeli, and the brothers gladly accepted it. Francis, however, insisted on giving the monks a basket of fish a year to pay the rent. In this way, the brothers wouldn't own any property and would have to depend only on God to provide for them.

These were beautiful times for Francis, happy days, when he and the brothers could follow closely the path traced in the Gospel. More men continued to join them—

Brothers Rufino, Masseo, Juniper and Leo—all eager to follow Jesus as Francis did. And Francis was a good father to his spiritual sons.

One night the community was startled from sleep by loud wails. "I'm sick! I'm dying!"

Francis bounded from his cot. Carrying a candle, he crept through the dormitory in search of the sick brother. Following the sound of the cries, he found one of the newcomers sitting on the edge of his bed repeating over and over, "I'm dying! I'm dying!"

"Of what, Brother?" Francis questioned anxiously, placing his hand on the young man's forehead. "What are you dying of?"

"Hunger!" was the shouted reply.

Francis bit his lip to hide a smile. "Then come with me. Let's go have something to eat."

All of the brothers, roused from sleep by the commotion, joined Francis and the hungry brother in a midnight snack. They shared not only food that night, but a good laugh, too.

Francis ended the episode with some kind advice. "My Brothers, God doesn't expect impossible things from us." He smiled at the young brother who had caused the disturbance. "When we're hungry he wants us to eat. Just always do your best and be in peace. The Lord will take care of the rest."

Another time, when some of the brothers were feeling discouraged, Francis picked up two sticks from the ground and pretended to play the fiddle. He sang and danced until everyone was howling with laughter at his show. He laughed right along with them. "The moral of this story, good Brothers, is never be discouraged. There's no trouble that can't be overcome by prayer, obedience and the spirit of joy!"

When Francis wasn't praying, he was preaching. His words were always simple, so that no one had trouble understanding his message about Jesus. When Francis went to a church to preach, he usually carried a broom. Before beginning his sermon, he would open the doors and energetically sweep out the church. "What are you doing?" the people would ask in surprise. With a smile, Francis would reply, "The house of God must be kept neat and clean. Jesus lives here and we should never neglect him!"

People began to wonder about Francis. "Maybe he's a saint," some even said. More and more lay persons wanted to follow his way of life. Francis wrote a special Rule that would help them to live the Gospel more fully as married or single people. This was the beginning of the Secular Franciscan Order or "Third Order," as it was called at that time.

And what about women who wanted to become sisters and follow Francis's way of life? God had a plan for them, too....

20

The Revolution Continues...

"I'm going to follow Jesus as Francis does," the young noblewoman said with determination.

"But Clare, what will your family say?" the older woman asked in shock. "What will your uncle *do*?"

"Pacifica, you've worked for our family long enough," Clare laughed as they walked along. "You know exactly what the Offreduccio reaction will be. Mother will come to understand. Uncle Monaldo and the others will think I'm crazy—as they say Brother Francis is." Clare stopped short and looked back at the church. "After hearing him preach again today, I *know* Francis speaks and lives the truth. And I *know* Jesus is calling me to live as Francis and his brothers do."

It didn't matter to beautiful eighteen-year-old Clare that she was from one of the wealthiest families in Assisi. It didn't matter that everyone expected her to marry into another rich and noble family. She had already sold all of her inheritance and given the money away to the poor. The only one she desired to marry was Jesus—the Lord of lords and King of kings. And she was finally going to do it!

Late on the night of Palm Sunday in the year 1212, Clare slipped out a back door of her mansion. She would never return again. Out in the street, she met Pacifica, as they had planned. Together the two hurried down the hill and through the dark woods to the Chapel of Santa Maria degli Angeli. Francis and the brothers were waiting there.

Francis stood before the altar. "Lady Clare, do you wish to give yourself and all that you possess to Jesus?"

"Yes! With all my heart!" Clare answered in a clear, ringing voice. She knelt and began to remove her brilliant jewels, dropping them one by one into a small pouch held by a standing brother. Clare's long blond hair shone like gold against her exquisite scarlet gown. The dancing torchlight lit her up-turned face.

Another brother handed Francis a pair of scissors. The hushed chapel echoed with the sound of snipping as curls tumbled noise-lessly to the stone floor. Next Francis hand-ed Clare a rough, gray tunic, a knotted cord

*Clare's blond curls tumbled
noiselessly to the stone floor.*

and a black veil. She went out to a nearby hut to change into them. A few minutes later, Clare reappeared. She was barefooted and wearing her new habit—the sign that she had forever exchanged all riches and honor for the love of Jesus. Her smile was radiant. She had never looked more beautiful.

It was done. Francis's Second Order had been born. Just over two weeks later, Clare's younger sister Catherine, from then on known as Agnes, became the second to join the new Order. Later, their youngest sister Beatrice entered. So did their mother Ortolana. Little by little other women came too. Many were nobles. Some were peasants. They all lived and prayed and did joyful penance together as real sisters, following the Rule Francis had written for them. They called themselves the "Poor Ladies" and they lived at San Damiano's, which Francis and his brothers had renovated for them.

The gentle revolution Francis had started was gaining force....

21

DOUBLE DOSE

"Everyone below deck!" The captain's shouts were barely audible above the raging winds and threatening waves. "Bring down the sails!"

The captain signaled to one of the sailors. "Go below and see to those two brothers. They're not used to the sea, let alone a storm like this."

The mate was already scrambling down the narrow hatch when the captain shouted after him, "And tell them to pray!"

The musty hall was lit by one flickering candle. The door to the brothers' cabin banged back and forth, as the ship rolled with the waves.

"Brothers!" the sailor cried, "are you all right in there?"

The cabin door stopped its rattling, as a small figure grabbed it for balance.

"Yes, sir," Francis answered. "Can we be of any help?"

"The captain said to pray…. We've run into a bad gale."

Francis's reply was drowned out by a loud crash of water against the hull. The jolt threw them all to the floor.

As he struggled to regain his footing, the sailor yelled again, "Keep praying, Brothers!"

And pray they did! The storm continued throughout the day. Dusk fell and their situation grew worse. Water was seeping through the beams of the ship. Later that night, there was a resounding crash and the ship came to an abrupt halt. The captain's piercing whistle could be heard from the deck. That meant trouble! When the brothers heard the cracking of timbers and the rushing of water, they knew their worst fears had come true.... The tilting vessel was taking in water.

Francis and his companion hurried to the deck. The ship was lodged on a gigantic rock. But they knew that their prayers had been answered, because there, only a few hundred feet in the distance, was land!

So ended their attempt to bring their mission to Syria. Brother Francis and his friar companion now found themselves in the country of Slavonia, with no food, no money and no way to communicate their situation. The brothers could not speak the Slavic language and the Slavs spoke no Italian.

But Francis was always ready to pray and God seemed always ready to answer. They found a sailor in the city who agreed to smuggle them on board another ship bound for Italy.

The brothers were stowed away in a small area behind the barrels in the storage room. It was far from comfortable, but that didn't matter. They had managed to obtain just enough bread for the voyage. Everything was going fine, until one night, they heard the familiar sound of howling winds, drenching rain and raging seas. The younger brother was pale with fear as he turned to Francis.

"Is it possible that it's happening all over again?" he gasped.

Francis pretended not to understand. "Everything is possible with God," he answered calmly. "We need to have faith."

"I'm sorry, Father Francis," his companion whispered. "I know that God rescued us once. I know, too, that he can do it again."

A short time later, the stowaways were discovered.

"Look here, men!" a sailor snarled. "Extra cargo!"

"We're already miles off course and our rations are running out.... Let's throw them overboard! It'll be two less to feed!" another crewman shrieked.

Francis thought quickly. "Brother sailors," he said calmly. "God is our good Father. He will give us our daily bread. We just have to ask him. Look, here are a few loaves of bread we brought for the voyage. We'll share them with you."

The sailors laughed at the prospect of a couple of loaves of bread feeding the entire crew. But they were moved by the sincerity of the brothers and decided to keep them on board. The voyage continued safely. And God *did* provide. That little bit of bread *never did run out*.

22

SISTER BIRDS AND BROTHER WOLF

The unsuccessful voyage caused Francis serious doubts. Was this God's way of telling him that he should become a monk instead of a missionary preacher? Francis had to find out. "Brother Masseo," he directed, "please go ask Sister Clare and Brother Sylvester what they think God wants me to do." Francis knew Clare and Sylvester were close to God. He would trust their advice.

Soon enough, Masseo returned.

"Masseo, what does God want from me?" Francis anxiously questioned.

"Father Francis, both Brother Sylvester and Sister Clare gave me the same answer: 'God has not called you for yourself only, but for others, too. Continue to preach.'"

"Well, then, Masseo, let's go," came the spontaneous reply. Taking Brothers Masseo and Angelo along, Francis started off down the road.

"Wait for me here," motioned Francis. The two friars watched as their master approached the woods. His small figure was dwarfed by the towering trees. Raising his arms as if to embrace the forest, he called out, "My Sister Birds! Be grateful to God and praise him!"

Suddenly hundreds of birds, forming a dazzling array of color, began flocking to Francis. They perched on his shoulders, his arms, on the palms of his hands, and even on the cowl of his shabby gray habit. Strangely, the little birds remained silent and still. Francis continued to speak to them, "Be grateful, Sister Birds, for you neither sow nor reap, but God feeds you. See how freely you fly, how sweetly you sing, how beautiful are your coats of color. Your Creator has given you these. Praise Him. Be grateful for the high trees in which you build your nests. Love the good Lord and always be thankful for his gifts."

The birds cooed and fluttered their wings as though to answer "Yes." They seemed to understand every word Francis had spoken.

Francis saw the hand of God the Creator in everything, and his great love for his heavenly Father overflowed to all God's creatures. He saw everyone and everything as a part of the magnificent family of God.

This is why Francis could really call all creatures "brother" or "sister."

A story is also told about the neighboring town of Gubbio. A group of anxious citizens there once summoned Francis and asked for his help when a wolf was ravaging the village. The wild animal was destroying flocks and endangering the lives of the people. Not even the bravest farm hand dared to approach the wolf. Small, barefooted Francis walked up to the edge of the woods alone. Worried faces peered out of windows; excited hearts beat hard and fast. Suddenly, Francis stopped. Calmly, firmly, he called, "Brother Wolf! Come here!"

The large, gray animal slunk toward the little friar.

"Brother Wolf," Francis scolded, "I've heard many complaints about you. People tell me you've been killing the village flocks and frightening everyone. God made enough for us all to share. There's no reason for you to take what the Lord has provided for others." The wolf bowed his head. "From now on," Francis continued, "you are to go from door to door. I promise you that if you do as I say, the people of the village will feed you."

From then on, as Francis had advised him, the wolf went "begging" for his supper and peace was restored to the town of Gubbio.

23

"SECOND" CHRISTMAS

Sharp winds swirled the layers of soft, fresh snow and a glistening cluster of stars lit the velvet sky that blanketed Greccio. All was peaceful and still. It was Christmas Eve, 1223.

As candles in the village homes cast their dancing reflections, a lone light shone high up the mountain. Francis and his brothers were preparing for Midnight Mass. The scene was a cave "lent" for the occasion by a wealthy landowner, John Vellita. Signor Vellita himself was present. Francis had picked the spot carefully. The cave, he thought, was so much like the one Mary and Joseph had chosen some 1,200 years before.

Earlier that day, the brothers had brought in an ox and a donkey and had placed some hay under the small, homemade altar in the cave. Why celebrate Christmas Mass with animals in a cold, damp cave, some asked? "I want to see with my own eyes the poverty in which Christ our King was born," Francis replied in his quiet way.

All those present held lighted torches in honor of the Christ Child. The Mass finally began. All at once something strange and wonderful happened. Signor Vellita stared in disbelief, then glanced at the others to see if they saw what he saw. The expression on their faces told him they did! There, on the hay beneath the makeshift altar, lived and breathed the Infant Jesus! As the crowd knelt in stunned silence, Francis walked the few steps to the front of the cave. Kneeling reverently, he whispered, "Are you really there? Is it really you?" Francis smiled tenderly at the tiny Baby. And the Baby smiled back. No doubt remained in the friar's heart. It was Jesus! Francis picked up the Child and held him in his arms, his whole being seeming to glow. Still smiling, the Infant raised his little hand and stroked Francis's beard. It was the first Christmas all over again!

Ever since that wonderful night, Christians everywhere have, like Francis, joyfully set up nativity scenes in their homes and churches.

There were years of consolation for Francis and his brothers. But there were years of sorrow, too. Five of the brothers had been martyred for their preaching in Morocco. Others who had followed in their footsteps had also met unwilling listeners. Even when Francis journeyed to Egypt to preach to the Moslems, he found it impossible to remain long. Francis remembered those happy days when he had preached to his Sister Birds and Brother Wolf—at least they had listened. Believing himself to be a failure now, he wept. He returned to Italy, broken in health and suffering from a painful eye disease.

The bitter years were beginning. The man who had followed Jesus more closely than anyone before him had, would now also follow his Lord to Calvary.

24

THE SORROWFUL MYSTERIES

Bare feet kicked up little clouds of dust from the sun-scorched earth. Francis and five brothers were on their way to La Verna, a beautiful mountain not too far from Assisi. It was Francis's custom to spend forty days on the mountain in prayer and fasting before the feast of Saint Michael the Archangel.

"Let's rest for a few minutes," Francis invited as they finished their climb. He looked from friar to friar. These five were his most loyal followers. "My Brothers," he said earnestly, "be faithful! Keep the spirit of holy poverty shown us in the Gospel."

No one asked what he was thinking. They knew. As had happened to many holy founders of other religious congregations, Francis was saddened by a few in his Order who thought they knew better than he did. Of course they didn't want to abandon their vocation. But they did want to change things and soften their way of life a bit. And Francis felt this would ruin everything.

A few days later, after much prayer and thought, Francis called Brother Leo over. "Please, Leo, read me a passage of the Gospels. There I find answers to all my questions."

Brother Leo opened the book at random and read the first section his eyes fell upon. It was the description of the suffering and death of Jesus. Two more times the brother opened the book and two more times, without planning to, he opened to other passages on the suffering of Jesus.

Francis was silent. He seemed to be praying. Finally he looked up. "Brother Leo," he said quietly, "I feel that I will soon die...and I would like to get ready. I'll go to live across the stream and remain alone with God. Please, will you bring me bread and water each day?" Leo nodded yes, trying to hold back his tears. Francis went on, "But before you cross the bridge to bring me the food, call out to me with the first prayer of the Divine Office. Come over only if I answer you. Do you understand?" Leo nodded again.

For a month Francis continued his silent retreat, fasting on bread and water. One night, Brother Leo stopped as usual on the bridge and loudly called out the prayer,

"Oh, Lord, you will open my mouth." He waited for Francis to answer. No sound could be heard except the water running beneath the bridge.

Leo shouted louder, "Oh, Lord, you will open my mouth!" There was still no response.

The friar was worried. His first impulse was to run across the bridge. But Francis had given him strict orders. *Please let Father Francis be all right*, he prayed in his heart. Finally, anxiety and fear got the best of him and Leo raced across the bridge. As he reached the other side, he could hear a muffled voice coming from the direction of Francis's hut. Brother Leo hid in the shadow of a tree, scanning the area near the hut. Suddenly, he spotted the figure of Francis lying face down on the ground with his arms outstretched. Leo came nearer. He could hear Francis whispering, "Oh, God, who are you? And who am I but your worthless creature?"

As the brother bent closer, he accidentally snapped off a dead tree branch. The echo of the sound made his heart skip a beat. "Who's there?" Francis cried, rising from the ground.

"It—it's just me—Brother Leo."

"Brother Leo! What are you doing? Tell me now, what did you hear?"

The nervous brother mumbled the prayer he had overheard. "Please tell me what you meant by this prayer, Father Francis," he begged.

"Oh, little lamb of God, my brother," Francis smiled, "in the prayer you heard I understood two things—who God is...and who I am. Imagine, such a great God is concerned about me. How good he is!" Francis exclaimed, lifting his face toward heaven. Turning back to Leo, he said gently, "Now that I've explained the prayer, you may go in peace."

As Brother Leo backed away, Francis added, "Make sure not to cross the bridge again unless I answer you!"

Leo nodded.

25

IMAGE OF THE CRUCIFIED

On the night of September 14, 1224, the feast of the Exultation of the Holy Cross, Brother Leo once again called over the bridge without getting any response. But this time he was obedient. He didn't cross over.

Francis heard nothing. He was totally absorbed in prayer and in contemplating the suffering and death of Jesus. His deep meditation continued all through the night. Lying on the damp ground, he prayed, "Lord Jesus, let me share your pain! Give me your love!"

As he prayed, Francis looked up and saw a radiant figure, a crucified man with wings. The figure spoke to him. "You will not die a martyr's death as some of your sons have. You will be transformed, instead, into the living image of Jesus crucified."

Francis recognized the figure as being Jesus himself! What did it all mean? Suddenly, deep, bleeding wounds began to form on his hands, feet and side. Iron nails

*"Lord Jesus, let me share your pain!
Give me your love!"*

became visible in his hands and feet. The pains of his Master seared his body until it became a replica of the dying Christ. But with physical pain came an overpowering joy and peace. Somehow, there had been an exchange. Francis had exchanged the sorrows he carried in his own heart for the physical sufferings of Jesus himself!

From that time on, Francis bore what is called the *stigmata*, the wounds that Jesus suffered when he was crucified for our sins. Francis didn't want to tell anyone what had happened. But he couldn't hide his secret for long. One day, as Brother Leo was washing Francis's habit, he noticed that the sleeves, the hem and the sides were stained with blood. Francis had to tell him the truth.

At the end of September, Francis left La Verna. A borrowed donkey carried him slowly down the mountain. As he rode along, he kept his gaze fixed on La Verna. In his heart, he felt that this would be the last time he would ever see its beautiful green shrubs or hear the rippling creek or the singing of Sister Birds. And he was right.

News of Francis's stigmata spread quickly. Throngs of people lined the streets to catch a glimpse of him as he traveled back to the Chapel of Santa Maria degli Angeli. Lining the route were many of the same faces who had greeted him as he returned from his military "career" years before. Many who as children had laughed at the "crazy" beggar man now cried out, "Hail to the saint...our saint!"

Francis greeted them and quietly continued on with his brothers. Praises from the crowds didn't impress him, just as the insults people had once flung at him had never disturbed him.

"Blessed is that servant," he had once explained to his brothers, "who doesn't look upon himself as better when he is praised and exalted by people, than when he is thought miserable and worthless. Whatever a man is before God, that he is and nothing more."

26

"Welcome, Sister Death"

Two years passed. Francis's health continued to worsen. The brothers called in a doctor.

"A month...maybe," the doctor said, turning away from Francis's bed.

"A month," Francis repeated happily. "And then I'll be free to go home to my Master! What joy!"

Brother Elias, who was acting in place of Francis as Minister General of the Order, had finally convinced him to have his eye disease treated. But it was too late. This time Francis would not recover. He grew weaker day by day.

Assisi had been Francis's home, and it was there that he wished to die. Often during his illness he now asked his brothers to sing the prayer he had written, his "Canticle to Brother Sun." The words echoed through and around the tiny chapel of Santa Maria degli Angeli:

"Most high omnipotent good Lord, yours

are the praises, the glory, the honor, and all benediction,

To you alone, Most High, do they belong, And no man is worthy to mention you. Praised be you, my Lord, with all your creatures,

Especially the honored Brother Sun, who makes the day and illumines us through you.

And he who is beautiful and radiant with great splendor

Bears the sign of you, Most High One. Praised be you, my Lord, for Sister Moon and the stars.

You have formed them in heaven clear and precious and beautiful.

Praised be you, my Lord, for Brother Wind, and for the air and cloudy and clear and every kind of weather,

By which you sustain your creatures. Praised be you, my Lord, for Sister Water, which is very useful and humble and precious and pure.

Praised be you, my Lord, for Brother Fire, by whom you light the night.

He is beautiful and cheerful and powerful and strong.

Praised be you, my Lord, for our Sister Mother Earth,

Who sustains and governs us,

And produces various fruits with colored flowers and herbs of all kinds.

Praise and bless my Lord and give him thanks

And serve him with great humility."

Soon enough, Francis added a new verse:

"Praised be you, O Lord, for our Sister Bodily Death,

From whom no living man can escape.

Those who die in mortal sin are sorrowful. Blessed are those who have discovered your most holy will, for to them the second death can do no harm."

Although Francis, the "poor man of Assisi," had no material wealth to leave his spiritual sons, he wrote a last will and testament, passing on to his brothers the most precious gift he could give them, the Franciscan spirit. He prayed that each of his friars would choose Lady Poverty as his spouse—totally and for a lifetime. This "Lady" had always been the love of Francis's heart, and she had led him to follow Jesus in real freedom of spirit.

On Thursday, October 1, 1226, Francis lay dying in the clay hut behind the chapel. Bones protruded from his worn body. His pale, drawn lips smiled at the brothers, his dearest sons. His deep, sunken eyes squinted for a last glimpse of each of them.

"I bless all of you here, and all those to come," he murmured, straining to be heard. "I bless you as much as I can, and more than I can."

The brothers prayed and waited. Heaven and earth were fighting for their father. Heaven was calling him, but earth seemed to want to hold him back.

Friday, Francis awoke in great pain. "Read the Scriptures to me," he whispered. One of the brothers took the Gospel in his hands, his voice shaking as he read. It was the passage about Jesus washing the feet of his disciples. How appropriate it seemed now. Brother Angelo and Brother Leo sang the "Canticle of Brother Sun" at the request of Francis, who joined in on the last verse: "Praise be You, O Lord, for our Sister Bodily Death."

That Saturday, Francis asked to have his habit removed and to be laid on the chapel floor. This shocking way to spend his last hours was understood by his brothers. It was Francis's final tribute to his "Lady Poverty." His mother, Lady Pica, would have also understood. She would have seen in her son's complete poverty a prophetic fulfillment of his birth in the stable. Even his father, Pietro, would have understood. Before he died, Signor Bernardone had come to realize that in the humility of religious poverty, his son *had* become truly great. Pietro had finally understood that Francis's uncompromising imitation of the life of Jesus had led him to become completely detached from this world and made him worthy of the kingdom of heaven.

The light of day faded and evening fell quietly. Only Francis's heavy breathing broke the stillness of the darkened chapel. In a shaky voice, he intoned Psalm 142, a prayer that ends with the words: "Lead me forth from prison, that I may give thanks to your name. The just shall gather around me when you have been good to me."

The brothers kneeling around him prayed. Everything was silent. Jesus finally arrived in the little room to speak the last word of Francis's life… "Good and faithful servant...come and share your Master's joy." (Matthew 25:21).

Francis was declared a saint on July 16, 1228. We celebrate his feast day every year on October 4.

PRAYER

Saint Francis, you opened your heart to Jesus, and you weren't afraid to follow where he led you.

When you decided to really begin living the Gospel, you ran into challenges. Your father couldn't understand you. Some of your friends laughed. To choose to live poorly and simply like Jesus just wasn't what people expected you to do! But this choice made all the difference in your life. It brought you freedom, peace and joy. It allowed you to lead many people closer to God.

I know God has a plan for my life, too, Saint Francis. Help me to listen to him in prayer, so that I can find out what it is. No matter what I do in life, I want to live the Gospel like you did. I want to follow Jesus totally. Pray for me, Saint Francis.

Amen.

GLOSSARY

1. **Apennines**—a mountain range that runs through central Italy.

2. **Chivalry**—a term used to describe the qualities of a knight, which included: courage, fairness, kindness, respect for women and a concern for the protection of the poor.

3. **Compromise**—trying to find a balance between two different ways of doing or looking at things.

4. **Cowl**—a hood.

5. **Divine Office**—another name for the **Liturgy of the Hours**, which is the official, common prayer of the Catholic Church. When members of the Church pray the **Liturgy of the Hours**, they continue the prayer of Jesus by reciting the psalms as he did.

6. **Franciscans**—the name given to the followers of Francis of Assisi after his death.

7. **Herald**—a messenger.

8. **Hermit**—a person who lives alone, devoting himself or herself to prayer.

9. **Heresy**—a denial of a truth of the Catholic faith.

10. **Knight**—in medieval times, a man, usually of noble birth, who was given an honorary military title by the king or by another high-ranking lord. Knights also promised to observe a special code of conduct. (Please see **chivalry** above.)

11. **Lay person**—any member of the Catholic Church who is not a priest, deacon, religious brother or sister.

12. **Religious congregation**—a group of men or women who are consecrated or dedicated to God by the vows (or special promises) of poverty, chastity and obedience which they make. These persons live together and carry out some form of service for the people of God. A few examples of such service include prayer, caring for the sick and the poor, teaching, spreading the Gospel, and taking care of the elderly.

13. **Retreat**—a special time set aside for silence and more prayer.

14. **Signor**—"Mr." in Italian.

15. **Signora**—"Mrs." in Italian.

BOOKS & MEDIA

The Daughters of St. Paul operate book and media centers at the following addresses. Visit, call or write the one nearest you today, or find us on the World Wide Web, www.pauline.org.

CALIFORNIA
3908 Sepulveda Blvd, Culver City, CA 90230 — 310-397-8676
2640 Broadway Street, Redwood City, CA 94063 — 650-369-4230
5945 Balboa Avenue, San Diego, CA 92111 — 858-565-9181

FLORIDA
145 S.W. 107th Avenue, Miami, FL 33174 — 305-559-6715

HAWAII
1143 Bishop Street, Honolulu, HI 96813 — 808-521-2731
Neighbor Islands call: — 800-259-8463

ILLINOIS
172 North Michigan Avenue, Chicago, IL 60601 — 312-346-4228

LOUISIANA
4403 Veterans Blvd, Metairie, LA 70006 — 504-887-7631

MASSACHUSETTS
885 Providence Hwy, Dedham, MA 02026 — 781-326-5385

MISSOURI
9804 Watson Road, St. Louis, MO 63126 — 314-965-3512

NEW JERSEY
561 U.S. Route 1, Wick Plaza, Edison, NJ 08817 — 732-572-1200

NEW YORK
150 East 52nd Street, New York, NY 10022 — 212-754-1110

PENNSYLVANIA
9171-A Roosevelt Blvd, Philadelphia, PA 19114 — 215-676-9494

SOUTH CAROLINA
243 King Street, Charleston, SC 29401 — 843-577-0175

TENNESSEE
4811 Poplar Avenue, Memphis, TN 38117 — 901-761-2987

TEXAS
114 Main Plaza, San Antonio, TX 78205 — 210-224-8101

VIRGINIA
1025 King Street, Alexandria, VA 22314 — 703-549-3806

CANADA
3022 Dufferin Street, Toronto, Ontario, Canada M6B 3T5 — 416-781-9131

¡También somos su fuente para libros, videos y música en español!